WILDLIFE IN DANGER

BY VALERIE BODDEN

CREATIVE ☾ EDUCATION

Published by Creative Education
P.O. Box 227, Mankato, Minnesota 56002
Creative Education is an imprint of
The Creative Company
www.thecreativecompany.us

Design and production by The Design Lab
Art direction by Rita Marshall
Printed by Corporate Graphics in the
United States of America

Alamy (Bruce Farnsworth), Corbis (David
Higgs/Sygma, Zeng Nian), Dreamstime
(Mike Hollman), Getty Images (Gary Braasch,
Hugh Patrick Brown/Time & Life Pictures,
Joe McDonald, Jeff Rotman), iStockphoto
(Nicola Destefano, Joy Fera, Dirk Freder, John
Frink, Andy Gehrig, Alexander Hafemann,
Jeffrey Heyden-Kaye, Patty Jenks, Andreas
Kermann, Alan Lucas, Howard Sandler, John
Sigler, Paul Tessier, Simone Van Den Berg,
Duncan Walker, Clark Wheeler, Anna Yu)

Library of Congress
Cataloging-in-Publication Data
Bodden, Valerie.
Wildlife in danger / by Valerie Bodden.
p. cm. — (Earth issues)
Includes bibliographical references and index.
Summary: An examination of the endanger-
ment and extinction of certain animals, ex-
ploring how wildlife in general affects Earth's
biodiversity and balance, as well as how
animals contribute to a healthier planet.
ISBN 978-1-58341-987-8
1. Endangered species—Juvenile literature. 2.
Nature conservation—Juvenile literature. 3.
Nature—Effect of human beings on—Juvenile
literature. I. Title. II. Series.

QL83B63 2010
591.68—dc22   2009028055

CPSIA: 120109 PO1091
First Edition
9 8 7 6 5 4 3 2 1

Table of Contents

CHAPTER ONE

The Variety of Life 6

CHAPTER TWO

Biodiversity under Threat 14

CHAPTER THREE

Human Consequences 22

CHAPTER FOUR

Striking a Balance 32

Glossary 45

Bibliography 46

For Further Information 47

Index 48

Everything human beings need to survive—air to breathe, food to eat, water to drink—is found on Earth, and on Earth alone. Yet the very planet that sustains human life has come under threat because of human activities. Rivers are drying up as people divert water for their own use. Temperatures are warming as greenhouse gases such as carbon dioxide trap heat in the **atmosphere**. Species of plants and animals are disappearing as people destroy essential habitats. And the rate of many such changes appears to be accelerating. "If I had to use one word to describe the environmental state of the planet right now, I think I would say precarious," said population expert Robert Engelman. "It isn't doomed. It isn't certainly headed toward disaster. But it's in a very precarious situation right now."

One of the major threats to Earth's health is the loss of plant and animal species. In fact, many scientists believe that Earth is in the midst of a mass extinction crisis, during which thousands of species could disappear. Most scientists rank this as a more severe environmental threat than the more publicized problems of global warming pollution and global warming can be mitigated with careful effort, the loss of a species is irreversible. Once a plant or animal has gone extinct, it can never be brought back. But why are species going extinct? And does the extinction of species we have never heard of really affect us? Is there anything we can do to prevent extinction?

Nearly every square inch of Earth's surface—from the tops of the highest mountains to the depths of the deepest seas—teems with life. Some of that life is easy to see. Some, such as bacteria, is invisible to the naked eye. But it all makes up part of what scientists call Earth's biodiversity. Short for "biological diversity," the term biodiversity was coined in the 1980s and was formally defined by 1992's Convention on Biological Diversity as "the variability among living organisms from all sources … [including] diversity within species, between species, and of **ecosystems**." In other words, biodiversity refers to the variety of life on Earth.

CHAPTER ONE

The Variety of Life

As noted in the definition given by the Convention on Biological Diversity, one indication of biodiversity is diversity among species. A species refers to a group of organisms that can be distinguished from other organisms by their appearance, behavior, or **genetic** makeup. Among sexually reproducing organisms, the members of a species are further characterized by the ability to breed with one another. Some species can be further divided into subspecies, which are distinct groups that are genetically different from other members of the species but that can still breed with them. Often, distinct populations of species or subspecies live in different geographical regions.

No one knows exactly how many species of plants and animals Earth supports. To date, scientists have discovered between 1.5 and 1.8 million species of plants and animals, but they believe that this is only a fraction of the total number of species on Earth. Estimates of how many plants and animals have yet to be discovered vary widely, with some scientists estimating that there are around 3.6 million total species on Earth and others estimating

Ring-tailed lemurs represent 1 of the 22 species of lemur, all of which are native to Madagascar, an island off eastern Africa.

Since the California least tern was first declared to be an endangered species in 1972, its numbers have rebounded significantly.

that the total number of species could top 100 million. The majority of estimates range closer to 10 million.

Among those species that have been discovered, not all groups, or classes, have been equally studied. Scientists think they have discovered more than 90 percent of the world's species of **mammals**. Most birds, too, have probably been discovered, with a total of nearly 10,000 bird species existing in today's world. In general, smaller organisms have received less attention; as a result, many more of them probably remain undiscovered. For example, although nearly one million different insect species have been identified, some

scientists believe there may be 10 to 30 million species that remain unknown. Even among the plants and animals that have been discovered and named, scientists have studied only about 100,000 in depth. Although mammals make up less than one percent of all identified organisms, they are the best-researched group. Many other organisms remain relatively obscure, with little more known about them than their name and general appearance.

Because no one knows exactly how many species are on Earth, it is impossible to know how many species have gone extinct. According to the International Union for Conservation of

Formerly on the brink of extinction in most of the U.S., the bald eagle was removed from the list of endangered animals in 2007.

Into the Wild

Founded in 1948, the International Union for Conservation of Nature (IUCN) is the world's oldest and largest global environmental organization. Each year, volunteer scientists help the IUCN compile its Red List of Threatened Species, a report on the status of thousands of species of plants and animals. The Red List separates species into seven categories: extinct, extinct in the wild, critically endangered, endangered, vulnerable, near threatened, or least concern. In 2008, 717 species of animals were listed as extinct, 37 as extinct in the wild, 1,665 as critically endangered, 2,488 as endangered, 4,309 as vulnerable, 2,448 as near threatened, and 16,226 as least concern.

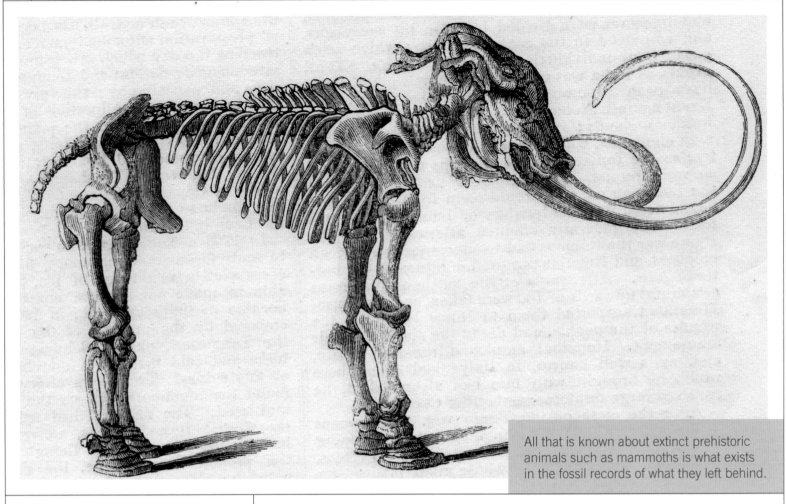

All that is known about extinct prehistoric animals such as mammoths is what exists in the fossil records of what they left behind.

Nature (IUCN), more than 700 animal species—including the Martinique parrot, the desert rat kangaroo, and the hula painted frog—are known to have died out. Many scientists believe that the actual number of extinctions is much higher, though, as many animals have likely disappeared from the planet without human knowledge, dying out before scientists could discover them.

Like estimates for the total number of species on Earth, estimates for the number of species that are becoming extinct each year vary widely. Some scientists believe that about 70 species permanently disappear from the earth every year. Others place the number much higher—between 3,000 and 70,000 species per year. Noted American biologist Edward O. Wilson estimates that about 27,000 species become extinct annually. Wilson helped to develop the area-species principle for determining extinction

Although his specialty was bugs, Edward O. Wilson's decades of biological studies focused on diversity within many species.

rates. The principle holds that, as the area of a habitat shrinks, the number of species it can support decreases according to a fairly predictable mathematical formula. For example, destroying 90 percent of a habitat will likely cause it to lose about half of its species. But if the final 10 percent of the habitat is destroyed, the species that survived the earlier habitat loss are likely to be decimated all at once.

Another way to determine the rate of species extinction is to look at the number of species that are currently listed as threatened or endangered and examine their prospects for survival. The definitive source for endangered species is the Red List of Threatened Species, which is published annually by the IUCN. In 2008, the Red List categorized more than 8,460 of the nearly 32,800 animal species it assessed as critically endangered, endangered,

Into the Wild

In Brazil, multiple conservation efforts are being mounted to save the golden lion tamarin, a bright orange, squirrel-sized monkey. Captive breeding programs have released more than 150 tamarins into the wild. Protected areas, such as the Poço das Antas Biological Reserve and the União Biological Reserve, have also been established. Strips of protected habitat are being planted to connect the reserves to other isolated fragments of tamarin habitat. In addition, educational programs are helping to increase local interest in conservation. Because of the combined efforts, the golden lion tamarin population has surged from fewer than 200 individuals in the early 1980s to more than 1,000 today.

The golden lion tamarin is named for its silky, golden hair and thick mane; it and the three other tamarin species are very rare.

or vulnerable to extinction. Among these animals were about 12 percent of birds, 21 percent of mammals, and 30 percent of amphibians. Some of the most critically endangered species, such as the Javan rhinoceros, the Iberian lynx, and the Bulmer's fruit bat, had fewer than 250 individuals left in the wild, putting them on the brink of extinction.

Endangered species are not distributed evenly around the globe. The majority of plants and animals under threat can be found in the world's tropical rainforests. This is largely because rainforests are home to more than half of all the world's known species. In addition, many of these species are specialized. That is, they eat only one type of food or live in only one small region. If that food source or that habitat is disrupted, these species are at high risk for extinction. The same threat faces endemic species—those that are native to a narrowly defined geographic region such as a specific island or mountain. In contrast, organisms living farther north or south of the equator tend to be more **adaptable**. They can eat more than one type of food and range over a wider area; if one source of food or habitat is destroyed, these organisms can rely on another food source or relocate to another area.

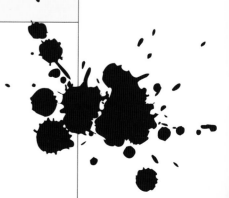

Although scientists acknowledge that extinction is a natural part of life on Earth, most believe that the extinction rate today is far greater than it would be without the destructive influence of human activities. As the human population has ballooned to an estimated 6.8 billion, human beings have exerted more pressure on Earth's resources, which, in turn, has threatened more species of plants and animals. The leading causes of species extinction today include habitat destruction, the spread of invasive species, pollution, and overharvesting. These threats rarely occur in isolation; a species that is threatened by habitat loss, for example, may also face competition from invasive species, which further lessens its chances for survival.

CHAPTER TWO

Biodiversity under Threat

Habitat loss or **degradation** is generally acknowledged to be the greatest threat to biodiversity today and is believed to contribute to the endangerment of more than half of all threatened species. Already, human activity has altered almost 50 percent of Earth's land surface, and the amount of area affected by human development continues to increase, especially in the Amazon basin, Southeast Asia, and eastern Africa. Even when entire habitats are not destroyed, fragmentation, or the breaking up of one larger habitat into several smaller pieces separated by human developments, isolates populations of species from one another, reducing their ability to breed and increasing their vulnerability to other threats. Such has been the case with the giant panda in China, which relies on bamboo forests for both habitat and food. Although pandas once roamed across most of southern and eastern China, all but a fraction of the country's bamboo forests have been removed, and pandas are today limited to no more than 20 small, isolated patches fragmented by agricultural development and a 2008 earthquake.

The IUCN estimates that there are fewer than 2,500 adult giant pandas remaining in the bamboo forests of central China.

In fact, agriculture is among the leading causes of habitat destruction and fragmentation. Every year, forests are cut down, grasslands are plowed over, and wetlands are drained to create room to grow more crops. Agriculture, combined with logging for timber and wood products, has resulted in a 20 percent decrease in Earth's forested areas, and each year, another 32 million acres (13 million ha)—an area larger than the state of Mississippi—of the planet's trees disappear, most of them in the species-rich tropics. Urban expansion, or the growth of cities, has also contributed to habitat destruction, with **infrastructure** developments such as roads, power plants, and water treatment systems rapidly taking over natural habitat in countries such as China, India, Mexico, and Brazil.

Along with habitat destruction, the introduction of non-native species is a major threat to many animals in certain habitats. Although in most cases new species are harmless, some can radically alter ecosystems by preying upon vulnerable native species or competing with them for food. Those species that cause harm in their new environment are referred to as invasive species. Sometimes, invasive species are intentionally introduced into a new environment. For example, pigs were first brought to Hawaii by Polynesian settlers in the fifth century A.D. Today, about 100,000 **feral** pigs roam the islands, eating the bark and roots of native plants and digging wallows, in which mosquitoes (another non-native species) breed. The mosquitoes carry a fatal disease called **avian malaria** to native birds. Other invasive species are unintentionally carried across the world on planes, in the **ballast** water of ships, in wooden pallets, or even on travelers' clothing.

Deforestation in tropical areas such as the Amazon is a serious threat to a wide variety of creatures, from insects to mammals.

Into the Wild

Although scientists have identified more than 1.5 million different kinds of plants and animals, the search for new species continues, with researchers discovering about 10,000 new species every year. Many of the new finds are insects; from 1999 to 2004, 260 new species of insect were found in the rainforests of Borneo alone. Indeed, many new species of all classes are found in remote rainforest locations, including two species of monkey recently discovered in Brazil. The oceans, too, are filled with newly discovered animals, including a species of deep-sea squid discovered in 2001 and a baleen whale identified in 2003.

Into the Wild

What we buy—or refuse to buy—can protect endangered species. Conservationists advise shoppers to avoid products made from parts of endangered species—such as turtle-shell jewelry or crocodile-skin leather. People purchasing an exotic bird, reptile, or fish as a pet should ensure that it was not captured in the wild. Foods containing palm oil (used in some processed cookies and crackers), which is grown on logged rainforest land, should be avoided, as should overharvested species of fish, such as swordfish. Eating sustainably harvested or farmed seafood such as catfish and tilapia, on the other hand, can help to reduce the fishing pressure on wild populations.

In addition to being overharvested, swordfish may also contain high levels of mercury, a substance that is dangerous to humans.

In addition to introducing foreign organisms into ecosystems, humans also often introduce foreign substances in the form of pollution. Aquatic species are especially vulnerable to the effects of pollutants such as chemicals, sewage, human medications, and agricultural fertilizers. In China, water pollution is so severe that 80 percent of the country's nearly 31,070 miles (50,000 km) of major rivers no longer support life. Some of the world's most dangerous pollutants—such as polychlorinated biphenyls, or PCBs (chemicals once used in flame retardants, adhesives, and other materials), and a **pesticide** called DDT—are known as persistent **organic** pollutants (POPs). POPs can travel long distances and remain in the environment for years; although many have been banned, their effects can still be felt today. They accumulate in the fatty tissue of animals, becoming concentrated in large predators such as polar bears and humans, and can affect the reproductive, nervous, and immune systems or even cause cancer.

Pollution also affects species indirectly through the process of global warming, in which greenhouse gases such as carbon dioxide (which is both naturally occurring and created by the burning of fossil fuels such as oil) trap heat in the atmosphere, leading to increased average temperatures on Earth's surface over the long term. Although scientists are divided over the extent and causes of global warming, some predict that the average temperature on Earth could increase by up to 7.2 °F (4.3 °C) by 2100. Changing temperatures may result in dramatic shifts in Earth's ecosystems, which may force species to move. Those that cannot leave quickly enough or those that need precise climatic conditions to survive may be wiped out.

In addition to indirect effects such as global warming, humans often directly affect species survival through activities such as over-harvesting. Although hunting and fishing on a modest scale rarely pose a threat to common species, overhunting and overfishing can

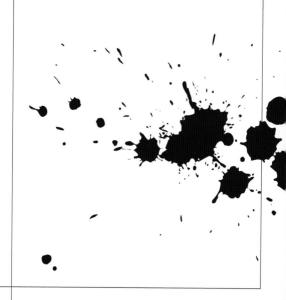

Gray wolves have been successfully reintroduced to many of the western and midwestern states in which they used to be common.

quickly lead to species decline. For example, the United States' gray wolf population was decimated in the mid-1800s because people feared the animals would kill livestock. In the oceans, many **fisheries** have been severely depleted by commercial fishing, and several species of fish and marine mammals have been unintentionally harmed as **by-catch**.

In order to protect endangered species from the effects of **overexploitation**, governments around the world agreed to abide by the Convention on International Trade in Endangered Species of Wild Fauna and Flora (CITES) in 1975. Despite the Convention's regulations, the worldwide trade in products made from endangered species continues and is today worth about $10 billion a year. Such illegal trade can include exotic pets captured from the wild, ivory produced from elephant tusks, and shark fins.

Today, Asia is one of the largest centers for the illegal animal trade. In China, eating rare animals such as turtles and salamanders is seen as a symbol of one's status. Traditional medicines made out of rhinoceros horn or tiger bone are in high demand in many Asian countries as well. A single pound (.45 kg) of tiger bones can be sold for $600, and a pelt can bring in an additional $10,000. Such a profit represents a huge increase over an individual's average salary in countries such as Myanmar, where most people live on less than $200 a year.

As people around the world move out of natural ecosystems and into cities, it can become difficult to see how the loss of plant and animal species affects human beings. But even though most people no longer live in forests and grasslands, the life in these ecosystems (and many others) has a direct impact on the quality of human life. From supplying products for direct human use to providing life-giving "ecosystem services," ecosystems and the plants and animals that live within them are vital to overall human health and well-being.

CHAPTER THREE

Human Consequences

According to the United Nations Environment Programme (UNEP), about 40 percent of the global economy is founded on products and processes from nature. Products such as cosmetics, clothing, food, and medicine come from the natural world. In fact, according to Niles Eldredge, a curator at the American Museum of Natural History, humans around the world rely on more than 40,000 species of plants, animals, fungi, and microbes on a daily basis. Among these species are those that we use for food, such as geese, salmon, and bison. Silkworms provide us with material for clothing. Horses and, in some places, camels supply a mode of transportation.

One of the most important products provided to human beings by Earth's plants and animals is medication. In the U.S., about half of the most popular prescription medications originate in the natural world. In the **developing world**, where such prescriptions are not always readily available, natural sources are still important. In fact, about 80 percent of all people in the developing world are believed to rely on traditional medications, derived chiefly from plants.

Today, camels are still used to transport goods and people across dry, barren stretches of land, especially in northern Africa.

Certain proteins present in cone snail venom are 10,000 times more effective than other painkilling drugs such as morphine.

Animals, too, have proven to be useful in curing human ailments. Venom from the Malayan pit viper is used to manufacture a drug to prevent heart attacks, and the anti-cancer drug trabectedin comes from the Caribbean **sea squirt**. Cone snails are a source of pain medication and may also have the potential to help treat diseases such as Lou Gehrig's, Alzheimer's, and Parkinson's. Scientists also believe that chemicals found in amphibians could be used in new painkillers and blood pressure medications.

Despite the human reliance on natural species for medications, only a tiny fraction of plants and animals have been studied thoroughly for their potential medicinal benefits. Scientists worry that if we don't work quickly enough to save endangered organisms, species that hold the key to new medical breakthroughs may go extinct before their healing qualities are discovered. Researchers' fears proved to be only too true in the case of Australia's gastric brooding frog, which was discovered in the 1980s. The frog's ability to raise its young in its stomach intrigued scientists, who theorized that chemicals secreted by tadpoles to keep their mother from digesting them might prove useful in treating people with **peptic ulcers**. However, before such a treatment could be discovered, the rare frogs became extinct.

Malayan pit viper venom is an effective anticoagulant, which means that it can help prevent and break up blood clots.

Plants and animals also supply the world's food. While the diet of much of the world's population consists largely of plant products, eight species of livestock, including cattle and pigs, also make up a major portion of the world's food supply. Each of these species of livestock can further be divided into a number of different breeds, with each breed exhibiting different characteristics; for example, some goat breeds produce large quantities of milk, while others are known for high-quality meat. As farmers focus on breeding more productive livestock, they often allow less productive breeds to become extinct, and every year, about 5 percent of the world's 7,600 livestock breeds are lost.

Every time a livestock breed becomes extinct, the gene pool of the world's livestock supply shrinks. Because the breeds that remain lack genetic diversity, a single disease outbreak or weather event, such as a drought or heat wave, can wipe out an entire population. **Indigenous** livestock breeds, in contrast, are usually better able to survive the climate extremes that plague their native regions. These livestock—many of which are decreasing in population as they are displaced by domestic breeds—could provide an important source of genetic diversity for domestic livestock. In many cases, farmers can achieve better long-term results by raising indigenous breeds rather than livestock imported from other regions.

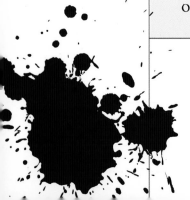

The more than 800 breeds of cattle found throughout the world likely originated with a single prehistoric species called the auroch.

When ruby-throated hummingbirds feed on nectar, their beaks rub against pollen, and they carry the pollen to the next flower.

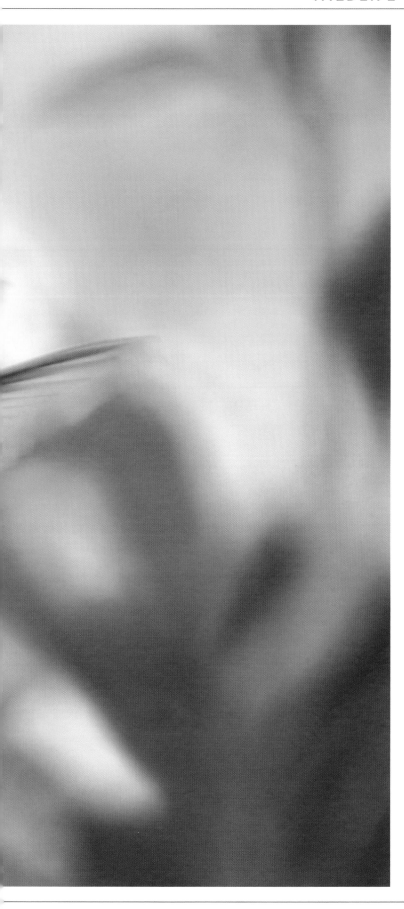

In addition to providing products for direct human use, many plant and animal species also help to regulate human surroundings and keep the planet habitable with their ecosystem services. Natural processes and resources supplied by the plants and animals that live within a given ecosystem produce oxygen, cycle and purify fresh water, and fertilize soil, among other things. Earthworms, for example, break up organic matter in soil, and their tunnels help to aerate the land, allowing for increased plant production across both natural ecosystems and farmlands.

Another ecosystem service provided by numerous species is pest control. Grazing animals such as goats help control weeds, and birds, amphibians, and reptiles reduce insect pests, including mosquitoes, which can spread diseases such as West Nile virus to humans. Other species, such as bees, beetles, butterflies, hummingbirds, and bats help to pollinate plants. Without such natural pest control and pollination services, the world could experience massive crop failures.

Although the loss of a single species may not affect ecosystem services overall, scientists cannot always be sure which species are vital to an ecosystem's continued functioning. According to the Millennium Ecosystem Assessment reports released by the United Nations in 2005 to assess "the consequences of ecosystem

Into the Wild

Of the world's 6,000 known amphibian species, nearly 2,000 are endangered, and more than 100 are believed to have gone extinct since the mid-20th century. Habitat loss, pollution, invasive species, overexploitation, and disease have all played a role in the amphibians' decline. Scientists are especially concerned about losing amphibians because these animals are considered nature's "canary in the mine." (Miners used to send canaries ahead of them into mines; if the canaries died, the miners knew the air was contaminated.) Amphibians are sensitive to environmental change, and scientists believe they may provide early warnings of what continued environmental degradation will eventually do to all species.

Native to the South American country of Ecuador, endangered phantasmal poison frogs are very small but carry a powerful poison in their skin.

One of the first signs of eutrophication is when a body of water such as a pond becomes covered with algae and other plants.

change for human well-being," the breakdown of key ecosystem services may very well result in the development of new diseases, changes in water quality, and regional climate change. Events such as **desertification**, floods, landslides, wildfires, **eutrophication**, and food shortages may also result from ecosystem degradation.

Beyond recognition of the vital products and services that plants and animals provide to human beings, many people believe that the world's various species should be appreciated and conserved for their **aesthetic** value. In addition, for many of the world's native peoples, such as the San (also known as Bushmen) of Africa and the Yanomami of South America, the natural world is an integral part of human culture and tradition. As the natural world is destroyed, these traditional cultures are also at risk of being lost.

The need to conserve and protect the world's wildlife first gained widespread acknowledgement in the 19th century, as writers such as Henry David Thoreau, John Muir, and Ralph Waldo Emerson drew attention to humanity's connection to nature and the need to conserve the natural world. Today, more and more people have become involved in the fight to save endangered species. At the same time, governments and nongovernmental organizations have recognized that they must find a way to balance human needs with those of nature and have sought ways to integrate development and conservation programs.

CHAPTER FOUR

Striking a Balance

One way that the international community has tried to control the threat to endangered species is through laws and agreements such as CITES, which included 175 member countries as of 2009. Few national governments besides the U.S. have strong wildlife protection laws, however. In the U.S., the Endangered Species Act protects wildlife by ensuring that citizens cannot "harass, harm, pursue, hunt, shoot, wound, kill, trap, capture, or collect" any species that the government has listed as endangered. Some people argue, however, that the law has exactly the opposite result from what was intended; because the government can prohibit the building of houses or the planting of crops on private lands on which endangered species are found, landowners are often motivated to remove such species from their property.

Since the beginning of the conservation movement, many individual species have been the focus of intense conservation efforts. Often, these efforts include captive breeding programs, in which a species is captured and bred in zoos or other facilities (where it is safe from the dangers of its native habitat) and

Leatherback turtles, which are critically endangered, lay their eggs on beaches and leave their hatchlings to fend for themselves.

Into the Wild

Although it may seem as though most endangered species live far away, many of the plants and animals near your own home may be threatened. But there are things you can do to help them. Plant your yard with native plants and trees and avoid the use of pesticides. Supply a clean source of fresh water. Provide log piles, dead trees, or weeds in your yard to serve as shelter for small creatures. If you live near a forest, help plant trees. Or, volunteer to help save endangered species in other habitats. For example, each summer, volunteers in the U.S. Virgin Islands help leatherback turtle hatchlings reach the sea.

Even if there is no extinction crisis, some animals that are extinct in the wild, such as China's Père David's deer, still need protection.

Into the Wild

Although 7 out of 10 biologists believe that the world is in the midst of a mass extinction crisis, others, such as Danish statistician Bjørn Lomborg, argue that the biodiversity crisis has been largely exaggerated. Lomborg points out that the known rate of extinction for the best-studied species—mammals and birds—is only one a year, making it unlikely that the world is annually losing the tens of thousands of species claimed by many conservationists. Others argue that human activities are not necessarily the cause of species loss or that ecosystems are fundamentally resilient and can recover from such extinctions without causing dire consequences to humanity.

Reintroduction of animals on a smaller scale occurs when an animal such as a hawk is released after being healed of an injury.

then reintroduced to the wild. Captive breeding has been effective for California condors, which became extinct in the wild in 1987. By 2006, 127 birds had been reintroduced in California, Arizona, and Baja California. Captive breeding isn't without its critics, however. Some people argue that animals that have been repeatedly handled by humans are not fit for reintroduction to the wild. Other scientists argue that conservation efforts are too often focused on individual species of "charismatic megafauna," or large, popular animals, at the expense of the small,

lesser-known species that are essential to the planet's health and are also in danger.

Because of this, many conservation organizations have shifted their focus from preserving single species to protecting entire ecosystems—and thereby saving the animals that live within them. One way to protect ecosystems is to establish conservation reserves, which restrict human activity or prohibit human entrance altogether. Today, more than 102,000 protected areas cover 12.5 percent of Earth's land surface—an area the size of India and China put together. (In contrast,

Lions are one of many animals protected in Africa's Serengeti National Park, which is part of a 7.4 million-acre (3 million ha) reserve.

Certain game reserves and national parks are home to stable populations of the five subspecies of endangered African wild dogs.

only one percent of marine ecosystems are protected.) Some scientists argue, however, that the majority of land reserves are too small and isolated to truly benefit endangered species; thus, they are working to build corridors, or strips of protected natural habitat, to connect fragmented lands. Unfortunately, conservation reserves often create hardships for human populations, especially in countries such as Kenya and Botswana, where people have sometimes been forced off their land to make way for reserves. Today, conservationists are taking the needs of the people who already live on the land into account when they develop new reserves. Between 2004 and 2008, for example, Myanmar's remote Hukawng Valley Wildlife Sanctuary was expanded to cover a

In the biodiversity hotspot of Madagascar, endangered, endemic animals such as Coquerel's sifaka are threatened by habitat loss.

total area of 8,000 square miles (20,700 sq km); it now includes five previously existing townships within its borders.

In working to conserve ecosystems, many scientists argue that conservationists' main focus should be on "hotspots," or highly threatened ecosystems that contain the richest diversity of species. These hotspots include the rainforests of Brazil, West Africa, Madagascar, Hawaii, and India; the Mediterranean-

Into the Wild

The Swiss-based World Wildlife Fund (WWF) is one of the world's best-known conservation organizations. Initially dedicated to preserving individual species, the organization's focus has shifted over the years to ecosystem conservation. Today, WWF concentrates on "ecoregions," or large areas of land or water characterized by similar species, ecosystems, and climatic conditions. The organization has identified and ranked the world's 238 most important ecoregions, dubbed the "Global 200." Unlike hotspots, the Global 200 ecoregions are not necessarily concentrated in the tropics but include such diverse landscapes as the Central Asian deserts, Canadian **boreal** forests, and Sudanian savannas.

climate **scrublands** of South Africa, southwestern Australia, and California; and the mountains of southwestern China. Although 25 of the "hottest" hotspots cover only 1.4 percent of Earth's land surface, they are home to more than 35 percent of the planet's known animal species.

One of the main reasons that some of the world's most threatened ecosystems are in danger is because they contain products, resources, and land that are valuable to humans. For this reason, some conservationists have begun to offer **incentives** that make the preservation of wildlife more valuable than its exploitation. In some cases, the incentives include direct financial assistance. For example, in a "debt-for-nature" swap, environmental organizations such as the Nature Conservancy pay off part of a country's bank debt, and the money the country saves is reinvested in conservation. In other cases, local communities are provided with schools, roads, or medical facilities by donors such as USAID in return for their support of conservation efforts.

Another new way to encourage local support of conservation efforts is to give control of the land to the communities that inhabit it. In African countries such as Zimbabwe, for example, villagers are allowed to manage the wildlife that lives on their land. Each season, the members of each village collectively decide how many elephants they will allow foreigners to hunt from their land; they then split the profits they make from the sale of hunting rights. Because the elephants bring value to the community, both the animals and their habitat are preserved, which has resulted in a doubling of the elephant population on Zimbabwe's communal lands.

Just as the people of Zimbabwe have preserved their wild lands in order to attract hunters, people in other threatened regions have begun to preserve their wild areas to attract "ecotourists," or visitors eager to see wild animals in their natural habitats. Although ecotourism is one of the fastest-growing segments of

When elephants are overpopulated or threatened in a particular area, they are sometimes relocated to reserves in other parts of Africa.

the worldwide tourism industry, some people argue that ecotourism dollars rarely benefit local communities, as most of the profit goes to paying international tour companies' fees. Others worry that ecotourism will generate an influx of vehicles, buildings, and other human disturbances that will further endanger species rather than protect them.

Despite the many conservation efforts that have been undertaken, some scientists fear that if human population and **consumption** continue to grow while habitats continue to shrink, up to half of all plant and animal species on Earth could be extinct by 2100. If, on the other hand, population growth is curbed, habitat destruction is slowed, and conservation efforts are stepped up, the same experts conclude that the loss may be held to 25 percent or less. Thus, the 21st century may be the pivotal turning point in the endangered species race. According to the UNEP, the choices governments and individuals make now will affect Earth's biodiversity for generations to come: "Our common future depends on our actions today, not tomorrow or some time in the future," the agency reported in its 2007 Global Environment Outlook report. Fortunately, people around the world have taken heed of this call to action and are working to ensure that wildlife will continue to roam our planet far into the future.

Into the Wild

Today, many ecotourism locations are working to reduce their impact on the environment in order to keep tourism from becoming another threat to wildlife. Tourists looking for an eco-friendly vacation can search the Eco-Index Sustainable Tourism Web site at http://eco-indextourism.org. Most of the vacation spots listed on the site are in Latin America, and all have been evaluated by an ecotourism certification program or recommended by a conservation organization. Among the resorts listed on the site are the Sachatamia Lodge in Ecuador, which sits on a private rainforest reserve, and the Weckso Lodge at the entrance to La Amistad International Park in the Panamanian rainforest.

Like its New Zealand relative the yellow-eyed penguin, the Galapagos penguin (pictured) is an endangered species sensitive to climate change.

Into the Wild

Some people, including former MIT political science professor Stephen Meyer, believed that the biodiversity crisis was over—and that the world's species had lost. In the mid-2000s, Meyer contended that no matter what humans did to try to preserve biodiversity, most of the world's species were simply doomed. This did not mean that there would be no life left on Earth; rather, only those species that do well in human environments—such as raccoons, dandelions, coyotes, rats, and white-tailed deer—would ultimately survive. Eventually, Meyer and others said, the whole planet could consist of **homogeneous** ecosystems, creating what they called a "planet of weeds."

The extremely adaptable raccoon, found most widely throughout North America, is one species about which scientists are not concerned.

Glossary

adaptable—able to adjust to new conditions or a new environment

aesthetic—relating to the appreciation of beauty

atmosphere—the layer of gases that surrounds Earth

avian malaria—a disease caused by parasites that is spread by mosquitoes to birds

ballast—heavy material, such as gravel or sand, carried in a ship to improve its stability

boreal—of the northern part of the world; characteristic of the cold region south of the Arctic that features forests of conifers and other trees such as birch and poplar

by-catch—the non-targeted fish caught by vessels fishing for a different species

consumption—the purchase and use of products and services

degradation—the process of breaking down or declining in quality

desertification—the process by which fertile land becomes drier and drier, eventually turning into a desert that supports little vegetation

developing world—having to do with the poorest countries of the world, which are generally characterized by a lack of health care, nutrition, education, and industry; most developing countries are in Africa, Asia, and Latin America

ecosystems—communities of organisms that depend on one another and interact with their environment

eutrophication—the process by which the excessive increase of nutrients in a body of water (typically due to runoff from the land) leads to the growth and eventual decomposition of plants, reducing oxygen in the water and leading to the death of animal life

feral—describing an animal or plant that was once domesticated but has become wild

fisheries—areas of a body of water where fish are caught, often for commercial purposes

genetic—having to do with genes, or the basic units of heredity that transmit traits or characteristics from parents to offspring

homogeneous—consisting of the same kinds of elements

incentives—things, such as money, that motivate people to take specific actions

indigenous—originating in a particular place

infrastructure—a society's basic physical structures and facilities, such as buildings and roads

mammals—warm-blooded, hairy animals that have a backbone and feed their young with milk from the mother's body

organic—derived from or relating to living matter

overexploitation—the excessive use of a resource to the point of causing it to almost disappear

peptic ulcers—sores in the lining of the digestive tract caused by an excess amount of stomach acid

pesticide—a substance used to kill insects or other living things that are harmful to certain plants or animals

scrublands—areas consisting of scrub vegetation, or low trees and shrubs

sea squirt—a marine animal with a baglike body that lacks a backbone and squirts water when disturbed

Bibliography

Anderson, Anthony, and Clinton Jenkins. *Applying Nature's Design: Corridors as a Strategy for Biodiversity Conservation*. New York: Columbia University Press, 2006.

Beattie, Andrew, and Paul Ehrlich. *Wild Solutions*.
New Haven, Conn.: Yale University Press, 2001.

Chivian, Eric, and Aaron Bernstein, eds. *Sustaining Life: How Human Health Depends on Biodiversity*. New York: Oxford University Press, 2008.

Eldredge, Niles. *Life in the Balance: Humanity and the Biodiversity Crisis*. Princeton, N.J.: Princeton University Press, 1998.

Meyer, Stephen M. *The End of the Wild*. Somerville, Mass.: Boston Review, 2006.

Stearns, Beverly Peterson, and Stephen Stearns. *Watching, from the Edge of Extinction*.
New Haven, Conn.: Yale University Press, 1999.

Wilson, Edward O. *The Diversity of Life*. New York: W. W. Norton, 1999.

———. *The Future of Life*. New York: Alfred A. Knopf, 2002.

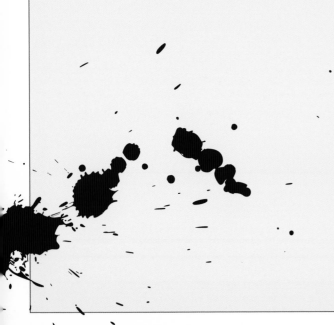

For Further Information

Books

Calhoun, Yael, ed. *Wildlife Protection*. Philadelphia: Chelsea House Publishers, 2005.

Libal, Angela, with Ida Walker. *Rural Teens and Nature: Conservation and Wildlife Rehabilitation*. Philadelphia: Mason Crest Publishers, 2008.

Redlin, Janice, ed. *Saving the Natural World*. New York: Weigl Publishers, 2007.

Vergoth, Karin, and Christopher Lampton. *Endangered Species*. New York: Franklin Watts, 1999.

Web Sites

American Museum of Natural History Presents OLogy: Biodiversity
http://www.amnh.org/ology/biodiversity

Biodiversity 911: Saving Life on Earth
http://www.biodiversity911.org

Conservation International: Biodiversity Hotspots
http://www.biodiversityhotspots.org/Pages/default.aspx

Dragonfly TV: Biodiversity
http://pbskids.org/dragonflytv/show/biodiversity.html

Index

A

aesthetic value of nature 31
Africa 13, 31, 39, 40
atmosphere 4, 19

B

biodiversity 6, 14, 35, 42, 44
  Convention on Biological
    Diversity 6
Brazil 12, 16, 17, 39

C

China 14, 16, 19, 21, 36, 40
conservation efforts 12, 18, 32, 33, 36,
    38, 39, 40, 42
  captive breeding programs 12, 32,
    36
  community control 40
  consumer awareness 18
  incentives given 40

E

ecosystems 6, 16, 19, 22, 29, 31, 35, 36,
    38, 39, 40, 43, 44
  and degradation 31
  protected by reserves 36, 38, 39, 40,
    43
  and services 29, 31
ecotourism 40, 42, 43
Eldredge, Niles 22
endangered species 11, 13, 18, 21, 24,
    30, 32, 33, 38, 42
  protected by laws 21, 32
    CITES 21, 32
    Endangered Species Act 32
  trade in 18, 21
endemic species 13
Engelman, Robert 4
extinct species 5, 10, 24, 26, 30, 36

extinction crisis 5, 35
extinction rates 10–11, 14

F

food supply 22, 26
  species used as 22, 26

G

giant pandas 14
global economy 22
  dependency on natural products 22
global warming 5, 19
golden lion tamarins 12
greenhouse gases 4, 19
  carbon dioxide 4, 19

H

habitats 11, 12, 13, 14, 16, 17, 30, 33,
    38, 39, 40, 42, 43
  destruction of 14, 16, 30, 42
  oceans 17
  tropical rainforests 13, 17, 43
human population 14, 42

I

India 16, 36, 39
International Union for Conservation
    of Nature (IUCN) 8, 9, 10, 11
  Red List categories 9, 11
invasive species 14, 16, 19, 30
  carried in ballast water 16
  introduced by people 16, 19

L

Lomborg, Bjørn 35

M

medications made from nature 22, 24
Meyer, Stephen 44

Myanmar 21, 38

N

numbers of species 6, 8, 9, 10, 13, 17,
    30, 35, 40
  amphibians 13, 30
  birds 8, 13
  insects 8, 17
  mammals 8, 13

O

overharvesting 14, 18, 19, 21
  by-catch 21

P

pollution 5, 14, 19, 30
  types of 19

T

traditional cultures and species 31

U

United Nations 22, 29, 42
  Environment Programme (UNEP)
    22, 42

W

Wilson, Edward O. 10
World Wildlife Fund 40